Text Copyright © [Success Publishing]

All rights reserved. No part of this guide may be reproduced in any form without permission in writing from the publisher except in the case of brief quotations embodied in critical articles or reviews.

Legal & Disclaimer

The information contained in this book and its contents is not designed to replace or take the place of any form of medical or professional advice; and is not meant to replace the need for independent medical, financial, legal or other professional advice or services, as may be required. The content and information in this book have been provided for educational and entertainment purposes only.

The content and information contained in this book have been compiled from sources deemed reliable, and it is accurate to the best of the Author's knowledge, information, and belief. However, the Author cannot guarantee its accuracy and validity and cannot be held liable for any errors and/or omissions. Further, changes are periodically made to this book as and when needed. Where appropriate and/or necessary, you must consult a professional (including but not limited to your doctor, attorney, financial advisor or such other professional advisor) before using any of the suggested remedies, techniques, or information in this book.

Upon using the contents and information contained in this book, you agree to hold harmless the Author from and against any damages, costs, and expenses, including any legal fees potentially resulting from the application of any of the information provided by this book. This disclaimer applies to any loss, damages or injury caused by the use and application, whether directly or indirectly, of any advice or information presented, whether for breach of contract, tort, negligence, personal injury, criminal intent, or under any other cause of action.

You agree to accept all risks of using the information presented inside this book.

You agree that by continuing to read this book, where appropriate and/or necessary, you shall consult a professional (including but not limited to your doctor, attorney, or financial advisor or such other advisor as needed) before using any of the suggested remedies, techniques, or information in this book.

e-Business Blueprint:

Your Pass to Financial Freedom

Table of Contents

INTRODUCTION 7

CHAPTER 1: REASONS FOR GETTING INTO AN ONLINE 8

BUSINESS 8

    GOODBYE TO TRAFFIC AND EARLY MORNING RUSH 8

    NO NEED PUTTING UP WITH A TOXIC BOSS 8

    WORKING AT YOUR OWN PACE AND TIME 9

    UNLIMITED INCOME POTENTIAL 9

    MINIMAL EXPENSES FOR AN OFFICE 10

    BIGGER CHANCE TO ACHIEVE MORE FOR LESS WORK 10

    COMMON PROBLEMS YOU WILL ENCOUNTER AT THE START OF YOUR ONLINE BUSINESS 10

        Tempting Opportunities and Resources 11

        Neglecting New Opportunities 11

        Doing Everything by Yourself 11

        Having Too Many Choices 11

        The Internet is Bigger than What you Think 12

        No Support from Family and Friend 12

CHAPTER 2: TURNING YOUR PASSION INTO PROFIT 13

    CHOOSE THE HOBBY TO START WITH 13

    DO SOME RESEARCH ON YOUR HOBBY 14

        Know the specific demand 14

    FOLLOW IT UP BY A MARKET RESEARCH 14

        Product 15

        Demand 16

        Competition 16

    CONDUCTING SWOT ANALYSIS 17

        Strengths 17

        Weaknesses 18

        Opportunities 18

        Threats 19

        The implication 20

    FORMULATE YOUR BUSINESS PLAN 20

    TRY SOME MARKET TESTING 20

- FINDING A UNIQUE SELLING PROPOSITION 21
  - Why do you Need to have a Unique Selling Proposition? 21
  - How to Develop a Unique Selling Proposition that Works 22
- **CHAPTER 3: GETTING THINGS READY – THE BUSINESS PLAN** 23
  - WHAT IS A BUSINESS PLAN? 23
  - GOAL SETTING 24
  - SET OF OBJECTIVES 24
- **CHAPTER 4: CREATING YOUR DOMAIN – THE WORKPLACE** 26
  - BUILD A PROFESSIONAL WEBSITE 26
  - FILL YOUR WEBSITE WITH USEFUL AND RELEVANT CONTENTS 26
  - YOUR WEBSITE IS YOUR ONLINE BROCHURE 27
  - TIPS IN REGISTERING YOUR DOMAIN 27
    - A Choice Between Keyword or Business Name 27
    - Consider Simplicity 28
    - Avoid Numbers 28
    - Location 28
    - Trademarks 29
- **CHAPTER 5: DEVELOPING YOUR BRAND – THE PRODUCT** 30
- **CHAPTER 6: BUILDING YOUR NETWORK – THE MARKET** 32
  - OFFER NEWSLETTER SUBSCRIPTION 32
    - Ask for Customers Opinions 33
  - MAINTAIN SUPERB EXCELLENT CUSTOMER SUPPORT AND SERVICE 33
    - Maintain a Fresh Website Content 34
    - Promote in Social Media Networks 34
- **CHAPTER 7: PROMOTING YOUR BUSINESS – ADVERTISING** 35
  - CREATING ONLINE PRESENCE 35
    - Creating a Professional Website 35
    - Use Local Listing Services 35
    - Invest in SEO 36
    - Advertise to your customer base 36
    - Utilize Social Media Networks 37
    - Send Out Press Releases 37

CONNECTING WITH CUSTOMERS	37
Writing a Blog	*37*
CHAPTER 8: MANAGING YOUR RESOURCES	**38**
TASK MANAGEMENT	38
DATA STORAGE AND FILE-SHARING	39
SOCIAL MEDIA SERVICES	40
SUPPORT AND USER FEEDBACK	42
CHAPTER 9: TIPS TO IMPROVE SALES PERFORMANCE	**44**
#1 - OFFER JUST ONE PRODUCT OR SERVICE ON YOUR HOME PAGE	44
#3 – PROMOTE WITH HOVER ADS	45
#4 – FEATURE PRODUCT BENEFITS IN YOUR HEADLINE	45
CHAPTER 10: ELEMENTS OF A SUCCESSFUL BUSINESS	**47**
CHOOSING THE RIGHT NICHE MARKET	47
CREATE A PROFESSIONAL WEBSITE	47
OFFER PRODUCTS OR SERVICES	47
GENERATE MORE CONVERSION	47
CREATE SYSTEM WITH TECHNOLOGY	48
CONCLUSION	**49**

Introduction

With an economic whiplash that hits the majority of the countries today; more people are joining ranks in achieving economic progress through the internet. The internet world had become an American Dream while others look at it as the other side of the world with the greener pasture.

Many had indeed taken their chance in starting an online business, yet not all are ready to face all the challenges and the complexities of surviving in the internet business arena.

However, for those who were lucky enough to survive, they lived to testify to the kind of life online business offers.

This eBook, "e-Business Blueprint: Your Pass to Financial Freedom" aims to provide beginners with a guide on setting up an online business and guiding you through the simple steps to achieve success.

With proper knowledge and determination, success on any online business can be achievable and in fact, rewarding. It's just a matter of planning and driving your towards a goal that can really make your dream comes true.

CHAPTER 1: Reasons for Getting Into an Online Business

People got different reasons for going into online business. But most often, online business is for people who got tired of working 8-5 or 9-6 every day. Rushing each morning for a gulp of coffee before fighting his way through traffic and hoping he could be earlier than usual!

As you realized that you are getting tired of working for someone else and you want to become your own boss, you start thinking of the possibility to make it big in the internet business. Hoping, you are right, and then the best way to set up a business with a greater chance to make it to success is to start now!

Here are just a few of the many reasons why you have to start with your internet business.

Goodbye to Traffic and Early Morning Rush

With an internet business, you don't need to rush up too early that you need to skip eating breakfast just so you can arrive in time for work. But when you are living in an overcrowded metropolis where you had to go through jam-packed traffic, stress and anxiety can be a daily part of your routine!

Online business can help you save a lot of money by not traveling every day. Count the savings you can have when you don't need to go out for work. You can likewise save your time and convert the time spent for daily trips into more productive inputs.

No Need Putting Up with a Toxic Boss

Most often people got fed up and want to get out of their work because they have a toxic person for a boss. Most often, bosses thought that their employees are there to please them all the time. This often happens when you are working in a sole proprietorship type of business or a one-man organization. Most often than not, you feed to your boss whims and schemes rather than get productive in your tasks. In the end, you feel thoroughly burnt out and find a quick way to change job.

Working at your own Pace and Time

When you are running an online business, you can be your own boss. You can work at a chosen time and place. You can even have more time to yourself and to your family. However, this can have its own drawback. So before you get out of your work, be sure your finances or the lack of will not cripple you. Proper timing is needed so your family will not suffer from your decision.

When you are free to decide for yourself whether you are going to work or not, be sure you manage your time effectively and efficiently. When you're alone to manage your time and no one is around to put pressure on you, you don't give yourself a reason to procrastinate. You need to learn to balance everything even without someone to answer to. Remember that every minute wasted is an opportunity lost in online business.

Unlimited Income Potential

Working on a regular career means putting up a cap on how much you can earn. But with online business, your ability to earn depends on how much time you want to put into your business. You can earn as much or as little as you want. The market for online business is too vast. You just learn to tap its unlimited resources and you go as far as you can.

You can target people around the world as the global market is getting bigger and bigger and more people are learning how to access the internet every day. You can work as much or as little as you choose. The marketplace for internet businesses is worldwide.

According to the later report of the Statistics portal, the number of internet users had risen up to 3.17 billion this year from 2.94 of the previous year. Isn't that market large enough to dip your toes into?

Minimal Expenses for an Office

Since you are working from the comfort of your home, you don't need to rent an office space. You will again be saving a lot on your administrative expenses compared if you are running a conventional type of business.

In setting up your business, all you need to have is your laptop or PC and low-cost hardware and software which you can even get for free online if you're just diligent enough to browse through your internet.

Bigger Chance to Achieve more for Less Work

An online business allows you to work fewer hours and achieve more. There are some business models that can be fully automated. You just have to set them up and (lo!), they can run on their own and earns you a passive income. This automation process now is widely used in the internet market. If you can't run your business on 100% automation, you can at least have it automated at 50% or more, so you can have more time for additional business to carry on.

What makes an online business unique than conventional ones is you can operate multiple businesses single-handedly. To simplify, you are operating a business that is almost next to impossible – Less capital, less time, and less effort for unlimited income streams potentials.

Common Problems you will Encounter at the Start of your Online Business

Starting your online business can be both rewarding and stimulating. However, you are sure to encounter a few problems that new entrepreneurs usually encounter. To steer clear of these issues, you must be aware of them and avoid them as they come along.

Tempting Opportunities and Resources

As you start hanging on the internet, you will be meeting a lot of opportunities along with remarkable resources to promising you great support in your online business. These products, usually software or a business opportunity, may be as great as their vendor advertise them. Nonetheless, if you jump from one opportunity to another, you will be losing your focus on your core business. It is, therefore, important that you start an online business with only what you absolutely need and have it run smoothly before getting into another. The same works with your software or any other tool.

Neglecting New Opportunities

Basically, this is the exact opposite of grabbing every opportunity that comes along. If you refuse to examine or look at any new opportunity sent your way because you have your focus set up trying to achieve a goal with a method that simply don't work, avoid overlooking the warning signs that tell you that you need to move on or move in another direction.

Doing Everything by Yourself

When you think it's better to keep all the profit, you keep trying to do everything so you can keep the money to yourself. Saving is always good for your business, but as your business develops, it will become impossible for you to embrace all the tasks. This is the time when you need to develop some way to ease up your workload. An example of these if subscribing for an auto responder that will take care of your mailing activities. Instead of manually sending letters, answering queries, the auto-responder allows you to maintain and develop relationships with your customer base and up-sell or cross-sell your products and services.

Having Too Many Choices

Affiliate marketing is a good start for an online business for you can earn as soon as someone buys from your inks. This is the reason why it is so popular with many people.

Affiliate marketing method has many positive aspects but there are too many choices that it is confusing to know which to promote. Before you jump into marketing a new software by way of an affiliate program, check how much commission you can earn from it, how you can get paid, and know if there is some support you can get from the owner. It is also important to know if the product actually sells before promoting it.

The Internet is Bigger than What you Think

Having an online business doesn't mean that people will naturally visit your website and buy things that you offer. The internet is such an enormous marketplace that you need to know how to get prospective customers to visit your visit so you can have the chance to convert these visits into sales. Meaning, you need to learn how to generate website traffic by utilizing both free and paid traffic generators.

No Support from Family and Friend

Sometimes, we presume that our family and friends will be our loyal customer. Sad to say, in most cases, it doesn't usually happen especially during the start of your business. There are even cases when they will discourage you from doing online business. Though these people mean well, don't get easily swayed and let your goals and efforts get destructed. If you have set your goal and created a business plan to back it up, you have every opportunity to get successful.

Regardless of whom you are, your age, gender, technical skills, educational background, you can always start your own internet business. You can always harness whatever skill you have through various learning platforms and resources provided on the internet for a certain fee or for free.

CHAPTER 2: Turning Your Passion into Profit

If there's one thing that really great with online business, it is the fact that it can revolve around your passion, skills and interest. Being new in the internet arena, you will be overwhelmed by the enormity of choice you can have in selecting what kind of business you can get into. As soon as you start connecting, making known to others that you are interested in getting into the business, hundreds of websites are just too eager to offer you choices. A new business is born almost every minute and the majority of them offer great potentials.

However, turning a hobby into a business is more likely to succeed because you are passionate and highly motivated to do things that interest you. How would you feel if you are being paid for something you want to do? Of course, one thing is sure here – you spend more time and effort doing something that you love to do. The same thing works in business. If you love doing the kind of business you have, then you enjoy every moment doing something for your business.

Some people fail in online business even before they can have their take off because they are not enjoying what they are doing. That's what makes it a difficult task. But if you are enjoying doing it, nothing is too heavy for you and before you realize it, you are done with it and have done it real good!

Your dream can turn into a frightening nightmare of responsibilities if you have not readied yourself before taking your course. So before you start getting any form of online business, try to take a reality test. Know if your hobby can realistically get you somewhere.

Choose the Hobby to Start With

You may have a lot of hobbies. This is good for you as it means, you have a lot of skills to go along with them. Nonetheless, you may get too overwhelmed. Choose one of your great preferences when you're still at the start of your business. You may choose the one where you excel best. Let's say you are good in selling anything. Then you know you can use that ability in a marketing business.

Do Some Research on your Hobby

As a business entrepreneur, you need to determine if there is an existing market for your particular line of interest, hobby or passion. It's not enough to go into business just because you love doing that particular task. Hence, if you love writing and you have that passion for writing anything, you have to know what others are doing to market this kind of skill.

Know the specific demand

By knowing what's trending, you will know what writing tasks are in demand in the market. If your passion is writing poems, definitely you know if there is a market for your poems. Maybe you can start your research with greeting cards publishers. You will also be able to find in your research available guidelines that you need to follow when you market your skill.

If you are good in marketing, this can be a good start for you. Marketing is highly in demand on the internet. You can start and join an affiliation marketing program and you can earn as soon as you are able to make a sale. Affiliation marketing programs are a potential source of income for beginners and don't need much of your time. You can even have them on the sideline.

Follow it up by a Market Research

When you are in marketing, you will realize that there is much competition out there. However, an in-depth market analysis of your products can help a lot to get you great head start. You may be new in the internet world, but marketing principles are still the same. The more knowledgeable you are with the product you are selling, the more edge you have against your competitors.

Having a marketing research should provide you data on the specifications of the product you are selling. People are very particular about the quality of the product and since there are more products of that kind available in the market, you must not disregard the quality.

Even if your service is excellent if the product is not good enough to provide customers satisfaction, you will not get a higher conversion rate for the product.

As you do your marketing research, gather information relative to the following.

Product

Determine the product standing or the company behind the product you intend to market. You can have an insight on the product by reading reviews and testimonies. Just make a search on the specific product and the search engine is quick enough to provide you with data relevant to your search.

Products are usually introduced or are being market by way of information campaign. You can read articles about them and how they perform to meet customer satisfaction but do not neglect to read comments of people you can find at the bottom of the articles. They will help you gauge the quality and performance of the product.

You will also read reviews provided by consumers and people who are in the same trade as you. Learn from them. One thing that is great with the internet is the fact that it allows you to directly interact with anyone even if you do not know them. When you can find articles regarding the product, interact with the publisher or other people who provide comments and opinions on the product.

Besides gaining enough knowledge on the product through the interaction, this can also be a great way to start a connection with these people. Contacts and connections are important in your marketing business or whatever business you will put up in the future.

Demand

As you browse on the internet for the specific product, and the search engine provides you with a glimpse on the relevant keywords, you will know if there is a specific market for the product. The existence of a market implies that there is an existing demand.

When there is great competition in a target market, it is because the product is highly in demand.

As an entrepreneur, choose a product with a big demand. You can also choose a product with average demand and lesser competition. When you can't compete with big and old-time marketers, and then opt for a possible product that is less competitive but can bring you great results. After all, a good marketer can sell even a bad spoiled tomato. Just don't forget nor bypass your principles of marketing. The word of mouth in marketing can still make or break a marketer.

Competition

Competition is like a school of fishes in an open sea. Just like you and me. There are too many people who are willing to take their shot at the abundance of the internet ocean and who would not? Given all the potentials and opportunities this world can offer, no one can fail to see what they are missing.

The competition is what creates you above the rest. There may be too many of you marketing the same piece of product, offering the same price and from the same source. But if you truly know what you are doing, having done some adequate research on the product and market before diving into the ocean of opportunities, then there's no reason for you to success.

Those who lose are those who procrastinates, cowards, and lazy. Others may not be that smart but their passion and motivation to learn and surpass every hindrance in their business are what makes them rise above others. You are one of these men if you have the quality of a hardworking ant, the meekness of the lamb, but the shrewdness of a serpent.

Conducting SWOT Analysis

If you are not aware of what a SWOT analysis is, it is an acronym for S - strengths, W – weaknesses, O – opportunities, and T – threats.

SWOT analysis is an essential tool in making situational analysis before getting into a business venture. This is assessing your business strengths, weaknesses, market opportunities, and threats through a very simple, logical process that can offer powerful insight into the potential and critical issues affecting your target market venture.

The SWOT analysis starts by listing an inventory of strengths and weakness. Note that this process forces you to focus on every aspect related to your business which you can't possibly do once you leap directly into business without any prior planning.

Identify the external threats and opportunities that can affect the business operation based on the market and overall business environment. You need not go over every detail but take the bullet points to begin with. Simply list down the factors which you think are significant to each of these four specific areas. You will still be reviewing everything that you have listed here as you work through with your business plan.

It is the primary purpose of your SWOT analysis to be able to determine and designate each individual factor, whether they have positive or negative significance, to each of the four groups. This process allows you to have an objective view of your business. This will be useful in confirming your goal and marketing strategy.

Strengths

Under this category, determine the positive attributes, both tangible and intangible relative to your business. Are they controllable? What are your resources and where do you excel most? What are your advantages over your competitors?

Strengths can include tangible resources available like capital, equipment (Computers, software, hardware, devices, etc.), existing contacts and social media memberships, and other online resources you can use in your business. Your strengths characterize the positive aspects internal to your business and likewise add value or offer you a competitive edge.

Weaknesses

Weaknesses are those factors that you can manipulate but can detract you from your ability to obtain or maintain an edge in a market competition. Which areas can you have greater potential for improvement.

Weaknesses can represent your lack of knowledge, lack of access or skills limited resources, technology or poor business location. These factors can be controllable but for a variety of reasons, need to be enhanced for the accomplishment of your marketing objectives.

Weaknesses place you at a competitive disadvantage while it represents the negative factors inherent in your business, detracting you from the value that you offer. Don't minimize or neglect existing weakness while making your SWOT analysis as factors in this category are greatly needed to enhance the best competition. Hence, the more accurate in determining and dealing with your weakness and limitations, the more significant the SWOT in your overall analysis or assessment.

Opportunities

Opportunities represent factors outside your business which poses as attractive potentials that give your business reasons to continue and prosper. Identify existing opportunities. Identify opportunities that are present in your market or in the environment which can be useful to you. Opportunities can be the result of market development, change in lifestyles, positive market forecast about your business, resolution of problems relevant to current situations, or the potential to offer greater worth that will create opportunities for your business.

- Opportunities include:
- Local and Global events
- Potential new uses of products and/or services
- Changes in technology and markets
- Changes in government policy or regulations/legislation in your favor
- Use of marketing or promotional techniques to boost the business
- Social factors such as population fluctuations, lifestyle, changes, etc.

The potentials somehow reflect the potential you can realize when implementing your marketing strategies. Expected opportunities that are inherent to the business and within your control can be classified as your strength.

Threats

What can intimidate your business operation? Threats are those factors which are not within your control. They can put your marketing strategy and the whole business at risk. Since they are external, you can't manipulate them. However, having contingency plans can help address them once they occur and threaten your business.

Factors that threaten your business are challenges created by an unfavorable market movements or growth that may lead to deteriorating revenues or profits. A major threat can be in the form of an existing or potential competition. Other threats are intolerable price hike mandated by suppliers, economic crisis, devastating media and press coverage, government regulation that can affect your sales, a change in consumer behavior causing your sales to decrease or an introduction of a new technology or innovation that can make your offers of products or services too obsolete.

Be sure to list down all factors that can prove to be a menace to your marketing efforts and lay all your nightmares on the table. They can be speculative but having them as mechanisms of your SWOT analysis can do a lot to help.

Classify these threats according to their seriousness and probability of occurrence. The more you are likely to identify potential threats, the easier for you to make proactive plans in response to these threats. You will need your SWOT analysis once you are face to face with them in your future operation.

The implication

The real value of the SWOT analysis is in bringing all the information with regard to the four factors together in assessing the most promising opportunities, and the most crucial issues.

The internal factors – strengths and weaknesses – in comparison to external factors – opportunities and strengths – can offer additional insights into the current standing and potential of the business. Let's say, how you could make use of your strengths to maneuver opportunities to your maximum advantage. Can you reverse the effects that threats can cause you if they turn out to be a reality?

Formulate your Business Plan

Formulating your business plan based on your conducted research and analysis is actually putting it down in writing. This will serve as your technical guide in the operation of your business.

Try some Market Testing

Once you had established what kind of products or services to offer, try to have a test of that product in the market. If you are a writer you would be launching soon a new book, try to give away some samples to some friends or loyal followers and have them post some reviews.

Through this, you will be able to get their reaction to the product before you have it fully launched in the market. If there are some negative reviews on it, try making some changes or improvements before finally launching the product.

Finding a Unique Selling Proposition

Because competition is something you must reckon with on the internet if you intend to achieve success, then you must find ways to position yourself in the lead. This means that you have to do more than just selling.

Just because you love to write, it does not necessarily mean that people will buy anything that you write. You had to establish yourself in the mind of the readers that you have previously sold bestseller books before you can do that.

A unique selling proposition is often overlooked but it is a very important element of creating a business that customers love. It defines your business unique position in the marketplace and sets you apart from competitors while actively focus your energy on catering to the needs of your specific target group of customers in a specific niche.

Why do you Need to have a Unique Selling Proposition?

In a great wave of competition, consumers usually find it hard to choose the one that is different from others – the one that deserves their trust, time, and money. Making the best selection can be daunting for consumers who don't have the experience to identify what separates one competitor from the rest.

As a good online business entrepreneur, it is your responsibility to help them by making a unique selling proposition that is obvious, different and easy to identify so they can quickly identify what your business has to offer that your competitors don't. In order to be easily remembered in a crowded competition, it helps that your business carries a trait that is worth remembering.

Differentiation is an important strategic and tactical activity. While a superior product and outstanding services are the major components of a growing online business, differentiation use as a competitive advantage can always make you stand out like a sore thumb.

How to Develop a Unique Selling Proposition that Works

The idea of a developing a unique selling proposition is not to work out to be the BEST but to be DIFFERENT. In a vast competition, working out to be the best will not set you apart from the rest. However, working out to be DIFFERENT will surely catch out people's interest.

Changing the rule of the game is the idea here. Competition won't be able to have its claws on you if you change the rule of the game. After all, people are commonly after something that is NEW and UNIQUE. If you can introduce a new game, the better it is for them.

CHAPTER 3: Getting Things Ready – The Business Plan

As soon as you are ready and strongly convinced that you want to put up an online business, you have to start formulating your business plan. The business plan can serve as your guide as you go along the way.

Without a business plan to guide you, you will be engulfed in the vastness of the internet world. Every business needs to have a business plan in order to be successful. It doesn't matter if it is online or a tangible company that is manned with a large manpower.

Before you get yourself into a certain type of business, it is a must that you have enough knowledge of what you're letting yourself into. After all, you won't dare to go somewhere you are in total ignorance. Fear and anxiety arise when you are in the dark and sure enough, you don't want any of these to happen to you.

Formulating a business plan at the start will force you to seek knowledge related to the business you have chosen. The first thing you want to know of course is if you can really earn something out of this online business.

What is a Business Plan?

A business plan is everything about your business, conceptualized and written down to give a more detailed and distinct quality. You need to put down everything in writing so you will remember details and will not get lost along the way. By doing your business plan, you are forced to think objectively about the details that are necessary for the operation of your business.

When you fail to think about the operation of your business no matter how simple it can be, you will soon find it hard to   things that you failed to recognize earlier. There are important details that need to be taken care of in business before actually getting into operations.

Goal Setting

The minute you consider doing a business, you start setting up a goal. It will serve as your driving factor that will motivate you to achieve success. When there is a specific goal set before any competition, every player's focus, action and determination are solely on that goal. Any distraction away from it will lessen your chance to bring home the bacon.

The same method applies to business, focus on it and don't be distracted by anything, not even by your competitors. Your ability to maintain a cool presence regardless of the existing condition is what makes you a perfect entrepreneur. Without a goal to which you can have your focus to is difficult.

Set of objectives

To back up your goal which is long-term in nature, provide a set of objectives which you need to achieve in a shorter term. These objectives aim to guide and assist you on some things that you need to accomplish in a certain period of time in support of the goal you want to achieve.

For instance, when you are still at the initial stage of your business, your objective is set on surviving. However, as the business grows and begins to win a share in the market, the objective is more likely to shift and geared towards expansion and boosting profit.

Now, being newbies to online business, you need to develop a set of goals for your business. The best objectives are set towards following the SMART principle.

- **S – specific**

It needs to be clearly stated and well-defined. An example is "to increase profit".

- **M – measurable**

It must be measurable with the desired outcome that is a number value that can be measured. An example is "to increase profit by at least 10 percent".

- **A – attainable**

Be sure that the objective that you have set is not impossible. When an objective is attainable, then you are driven to work it out in the soonest possible time. But when you know it is impossible, no amount of time, effort, or investment can turn it into a reality.

- **R- realistic**

Given the possible resources like the financial resources available and with your available skill, time, and effort, the target is becoming possible.

- **T – time bound**

The objective that you set is expected to be completed within a specific schedule or within a given period of time. Let's say within a 12-month timeframe.

Smart objectives allow you to assess your performance from time to time and make adjustments for better improvement.

CHAPTER 4: Creating Your Domain – The Workplace

When you are starting your business, you consider your workplace among other things.

Your workplace is actually a representation of who you are, so make sure it represents the good and nice sides of you. It is where you start your business and it where customers expect to find your products. Your workplace showcases everything that one wants to know and see in you.

In the internet world, your domain is your workplace and your showground. When you set up your business, this is where you need to get a fresh start.

If you are serious about online business, then you have to create your domain. A domain is your business address. An example of a domain is yahoo.com for the sake of those who are new to the internet and don't know what a domain is.

Build a Professional Website

Your business as we have stated previously stated can be based on your hobby but having a professional-looking website is important if you want your business to succeed. Being a beginner, you may not realize this, but the appropriate domain is important to your success on the internet.

Having a website that does not look professional will have its bad impact on your business. So if at first, you don't have the capability to create a website that can't reflect the kind of business personality you want to emit, then, have it done by a professional web designer. You need to have a website that can totally knock out every viewer and send them pulling out their credit cards.

Fill your Website with Useful and Relevant Contents

You may come across an internet adage that says, "Content is King." This is because internet users prefer to indulge their viewing time on useful contents that arouse human interest. Hence, the only way to have viewers flocked and stay longer on your website and later purchased some products are through your contents.

Make sure that your contents are relevant to your site. Your niche chooses the kind of contents that should stay there. Search engines like Google, Yahoo, and Bing are very strict with their rules regarding relevant contents.

Websites that fail to follow their rules and regulations regarding this will face penalties even before they know it.

Your Website is your Online Brochure

Use your website as an online brochure for your products and services offered to customers. Since your website will showcase all your products and services, you have to make sure that all pages are easy to navigate and comprehensible. Viewer won't waste their precious time waiting while your site is loading. Same thing that they won't stay long enough if your content is not easy to read and understand.

Tips in Registering your Domain

You have to consider a lot of things in registering your domain name. To guide you on this, here are some valuable tips. Once you have settled on a domain name, it is quite difficult to change it.

A Choice Between Keyword or Business Name

In choosing a name, some people would choose between a keyword or a business name?

There are always pros and cons in having your choices. When your keyword is relevant to your site niche, it will rank better and a viewer is more likely to search for keywords in searching for a product they want to buy or on a certain topic they want to read rather than search for a brand name when they had never heard of it before. Domain names using keywords are great for websites dedicated to a particular theme or subject. However, since a lot of people are after keywords, it could be quite hard to register some keyword choices. Most of the best keywords are most often taken or registered.

Keywords are not also applicable when you intend to sell multiple products or if you wish to enhance your business in the future and keywords will no longer be relevant then.

On the other hand, when you are registering your domain name using your business name, then you are open to selling any products or services you want. You can even make a shift from what you are starting when in the future; you find your plans not working well with your present offers.

Consider Simplicity

No matter what way you choose in your name selection, make sure that it is simple, easy to recognize and remember. Short names are quick to remember than long ones. Domain names that are memorable are also easy to remember. Some prefer unique but short domain names to create interest and leave something in people's memory.

Avoid Numbers

If you use numbers in your domain name, people aren't really trying to figure out if you are using the number in figures or in the word. This makes it hard to remember, so better to stay away from choosing a number name.

Location

If you prefer running a business in a specific geographical location, then try to include the location in your domain name as long as it does not complicate the whole thing.

Trademarks

Be sure that the name you are choosing for your domain is not yet trademarked by someone else. You can be in a lot of trouble if you did not and find out later that it had been trademarked by another.

In addition, here are some final tips.

Keep your domain name easy to spell. Those that are often times misspelled are also hard to remember. Viewers are not willing to spend time trying to remember the correct spelling and would rather search for other sites as well.

Never use hyphenated domain names as they are not easy to remember and may not rank well with search engines.

As much as possible, stick to the .com domain as people often remember this compared to other domain extensions.

Lastly, don't just register the domain name you had chosen but also register a number of variations of the name. This will ensure that others are prevented from registering similar names. Doing it this way won't cost you too much and you can always redirect then so that traffic on those sites will redirect to your main website.

CHAPTER 5: Developing your Brand – The Product

When you are selling something, may it be a product or a service that you offer, branding is important. It can be a name, term, design or symbol, logo or any combination of these elements that identify the products or the services. These elements are unique and distinguished them from other sellers.

When you are on online business, it is important that you brand yourself as the owner of the site or as an authority on the niche aside from the product. Because trust is important in building a relationship with your customer base, it is relatively important that your customers know you and they can interact with you as well. In other words, the more visible you are to the public, the more than you will be able to gain their trust and confidence.

In the internet arena, people are more likely to buy your product at first because of you and not because of the product itself. This is why branding is important as it pulls people towards you.

As you are establishing a name for your website, you are also establishing a name for yourself on the internet. Branding is not only encouraging your target market to choose you over your competitors but it is also getting your prospects see you as the sole provider of the solution to their problem or need.

Visibility is a must if you want to be remembered by. This is why you need to maintain a regular blog to keep in touch with your viewers. Blogging is a good way of talking about your products and service, informing people of how they are useful to them and at the same time, letting your viewers know things about you.

When your viewer can trust you with your ideas and you were able to gain their trust and confidence, you can see that their visits are converted into sales.

A good brand aims to establish the following across the internet:

- Clearly deliver the message you are sending

- Emotionally relate your prospects and potential customers to your products and services
- Confirms your credibility
- Motivates buyers to purchase your products or hire your services.
- Creates customers loyalty

To be effective in branding, you must understand the needs and wants of your customers, both loyal and potential. This is achieved by integrating your brand strategies at every point of public contact. It is imperative that you must think of branding as an expression of who you are as a representation of your business and what you offer.

When consumers begin to identify with you, your brand will live within the hearts and minds. Branding is the totality of their experiences and perceptions, some of which you can influence. As competition for customers intensify day by day, it is important to spend more time investing in researching, building and defining your brand. After all, your brand is your promise to your customers.

The brand is a major component of your marketing communication and one you don't want to be without. Your brand serves as a guide to understanding the purpose of business objectives while it enables you to align a marketing plan with those objectives and fulfill overall business strategy.

A brand's effectiveness does not happen before the purchase; however, it's about the life of the brand and the experience it gives the customers. A good brand must be able to answer the following:

- Did the product or service perform as expected?
- Was the quality as good as promised?
- How was the service experienced?

If you get positive answers to the above questions, then you've got loyal customers.

CHAPTER 6: Building Your Network – The Market

As a beginner in online business, one of your main concerns is building your customer base as it will serve as your market for products and services you are offering. This is a hard task to begin with as people buy only from the business they trust.

To increase your customer base, it is imperative to be constantly visible and stay in contact with potential and existing customers while offering more value to customers. This way, they will likely remain to be loyal. However, you need a 5% increase in customer retention to have 75% increase result in customer value. So the problem lies on how to improve your customer retention by 5 percent.

Here are some ways to bring in more customers in order for you to increase your customer base.

Offer Newsletter Subscription

Offering subscriptions like newsletters is a way of getting regular contact with your customer base. This is also a great way of building your mail list which is the core of every marketing campaign. As a marketer would commonly say, "Money is on the list," inviting your viewers to sign up for a newsletter subscription will do you many good things.

You can easily connect your sign up page to your mailing list and/or responder to make things easy for. An example of this is the Mail chimp which is for free while you are still starting to gather your first 2,000 subscriptions. After that, you will be paying a minimal amount per month to continue with their services.

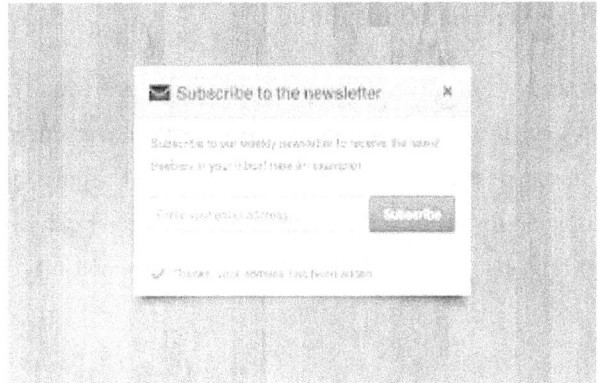

Ask for Customers Opinions

Before a viewer leaves your website, ask them to leave a comment or their opinion either on the product, service or their experience. They are just too happy to have their say on anything. This is one way of interacting with your customer and telling them that you care. While you hear them and see their point of views, you can improve the value of your products and services as well as your customer's value. You may also use short and simple surveys to conduct industry research, customers experience and customer satisfaction.

Maintain Superb Excellent Customer Support and Service

A customer who contacts customer support is someone who truly valued your product and service rather than the one who just turns away without telling you how they feel about the product or service. By giving the kind of service that the customers expect from you or by simply taking an action, you can expect a loyal customer out of this one. And maybe not just one for that kind of customer can always pass a recommendation to others, thus, helping your increase your customer base. A satisfied ad delighted customer can always lead to more sales and recommendations.

Maintain a Fresh Website Content

The fresh and informative content of a website are what draw new visitors to it. From among these visitors, you can have your potential customers so make it a habit of posting fresh content or regularly publishing a blog that reports current business news, hot items and topics relevant to your niche or maybe some ticklers to keep your business alive. Fresh content also allows your website more opportunity to be found in search engines.

Promote in Social Media Networks

Promoting through the social media is the fastest and the easiest way to have your business across the world. An average number of friends that a Facebook user can have are more than two hundred. When you publish a new blog, run a new campaign or launch a new product, the least that you can do is to share it with your friends in social media who in return would share them with others. In lesser time than when you actually promote offline, you can easily reach out to a large number of groups. Just make sure that you deliver useful and interesting content to motivate others to share and re-share them. Isn't this a great way to grow your customer base?

Remember that in social media, you have your own set of friends or contacts, which also have their own set of connections. You can not only reach to your own network but you can, in fact, connect with your friends' own networks and so on. It is an expandable network frame. If you want to reach out to more people, simply add more friends and you can grow them large enough to expand your customer base.

CHAPTER 7: Promoting your Business – Advertising

Everyone knows what a good advertising can do to promote a business-physical or online.

Advertising is an essential tool in marketing. Even if you have the best product and services, you just can't rely alone on the word of mouth or recommendations. It is not enough to keep your online business thrives against the multitudes of competitors.

In today's market, you have to establish an online presence to reach a large customer base and connect with consumers.

Creating Online Presence

Creating a Professional Website

Just as we have previously discussed in other chapters prior to this one, you will need at least one professional website to showcase your product, create your brand and connect with your customer base and potential customers. This is where you are to focus your efforts on improving your business.

Use Local Listing Services

To attract local business, sign up for services like Google Maps or local Yahoo searches that are currently operating like Google, Yahoo or Bing.

Aside from getting you listed on these directories and making your business available for searches, these services also allow you to post photos and graphics, real-time updates and other information like parking tips. They likewise allow customers to post previews of business and to top it all, they are for FREE.

Invest in SEO

As a beginner, you may not easily understand what SEO is all about. SEO is short for Search Engine Optimization. By optimizing your search engine tools and requirements, major search engines will include your webpage on the first few pages of search results.

You may ask why you need to be on any of these first few pages. The answer is simple. When you are a user, you usually start searching for information that you need in the search engine's search bar. You can find this on your browser near the magnifying glass icon. As you search using keywords, the search engine will then find them for you and bring you to the first page of the search result. From there, you may find what you're searching for through browsing different pages. If your page happens to be one of them, only then can your website page be viewed. Since your sales rely on your viewers, you need more viewers to your page. To do this, you need to invest in your SEO as part of your marketing and advertising strategies.

If you are a business owner, even if you happen to be a newcomer in online business, then you probably understand what good advertising can do to your business. As a business entrepreneur, you would like many people to know about your merchandise and services and where to exactly find them. This is applicable to both online and offline business.

Other ways to optimize your website include writing interesting, useful and relevant content, using tags and posting images so people who are using image searches are brought to your website.

Advertise to your customer base

Online advertising is generally costly especially if intended to reach large groups of people. By targeting your advertisement, you will be able to attract the type of traffic you want to your website.

There are online services that display your advertisement to customers in relevant websites and those who make relevant searches. This will likely increase the chances that viewers of your ad will actually click through it. An example of these online services is Google AdWords. There are also other search engines that offer this kind of service. However, you may search for free advertising. There are lots of free websites offering this service including Adboards, Craig's list, Backpages, etc.

Another way to advertise to your customer base is to connect with websites that are not your direct competitors and see if they allow trading website ads. If they allow you to post some ads on their websites, they will also post some of their ads on yours.

Utilize Social Media Networks

Social Media Networks like Twitter, Facebook, LinkedIn and Pinterest have become a necessary tool for doing business. Take time to join on these free social media sites and create interesting profiles or community pages on each of these platforms.

Send Out Press Releases

This can be a great way of getting your ads published on targeted and widely read publications. You can have a press release when you're launching a new product or announcing a sales record to create a good public image for your business.

Connecting with Customers

Writing a Blog

Maintain a blog especially an interesting one and you can draw and keep customers in by way of involving them in your business. It is necessary to post regularly if not daily especially for a beginner like you to hold customers attention.

CHAPTER 8: Managing your Resources

The very basic of all resources that we have is time. Working online may give a leeway of your time but it doesn't mean you can have more time for leisure and recreation. You need more time online that what you really think. Though there's no one to require you to spend more time, the vast opportunities make it possible that you will need more time that you expect.

To be able to manage your time and spend it productively, you need to avail of some resources – tools and apps that you can use to manage your resources – especially time and effort. But what tools are most helpful when you are getting started?

We all know that most often, there are too many details that you need to remember and you can easily get lost in a labyrinth of choices. But you must take the time to provide the most benefit to your business.

Task Management

One problem you are likely to encounter is keeping everything organized. To keep things in proper order, you need to organize your task through a task management system. The internet provides countless solution an again this can be confusing. You will find it hard deciding which is the best. Everything will depend on what you are looking for and how much functionality is required.

Here are some of the management tools you may try and see if they can work great for you.

Asana – This works well with any type of company and has a simple interface. You can work on it alone or with your team. You can also invite others to work on it with some specific task. It is a great way to start using this task manager and you can avail of a free account while learning the use of its features.

Teambox - is another collaborating platform for managing tasks. It allows multiple project workspaces so you can organize tasks between different online products or even completely different companies. Teambox also includes an interactive feature where you can manage other members of your team.

Trello – It's another collaboration tool that comes with a free price tag. Trello organizes your projects into boards and tells you what's being worked on, who's working on something and if anything is still in process. Though it's simple and does not offer many features like in any other project management tools, the interface is more focused on tasks/project than on collaboration works.

Collaboration task can be an effort but online cloud hosting platforms make it much more easily with their file-sharing feature.

Data Storage and File-Sharing

Dropbox – If you want a powerful solution for keeping your files organized and easy sharing with other people, then you must consider using Dropbox. It offers a free plan with limited files for storage. However, you can add more to your storage space by upgrading your account by inviting others to join you on this platform. The interface is simple and easy as you can just drag and drop files to upload into your account. You can even download entire folders of content as .zip containers right from the website. It is indeed great for collaboration efforts.

Social Media Services

If you want to create an online presence especially when branding and promoting your products and services online, you need to register your own accounts in any or all of social networking sites that offer social media services like Facebook, Twitter, LinkedIn, VK, and so on…

Nonetheless, having too many social media sites means too much time and efforts need in managing these sites. To help you in these tasks, here are some tools to lighten your responsibilities.

GrabInBox – An easy way to manage multiple social networks accounts and quickly schedule messages on Facebook and twitter.

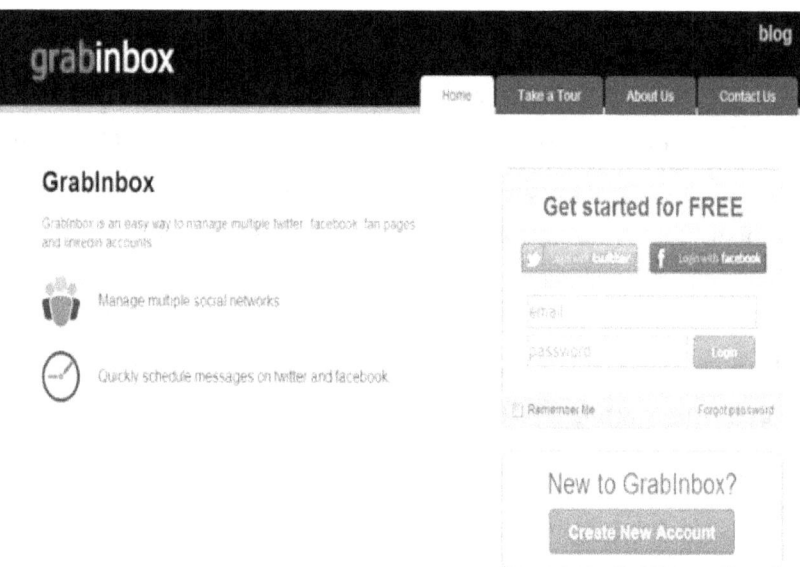

HootSuite – A proven professional solution with a free account. You can easily manage your social profiles from Twitter, GooglePlus, FaceBook, LinkedIn and much more.

UI/UX Testing – These stand for User Interface (UI) and User experience (UE). Bothe deals with the relationship of the product to its users. While User interface deals with the interaction between the user and the product, user experience deals with the sensitivity and reception to the users.

Browser Stack – Unluckily, service is not available for free but it's a great support for browser testing. You can easily create screenshots from any browser and saves you time in squashing bugs if your site is not rendering properly for a certain browser version. It also allows you to run tests on more complicated features like JavaScript or responsive CSS within legacy browsers.

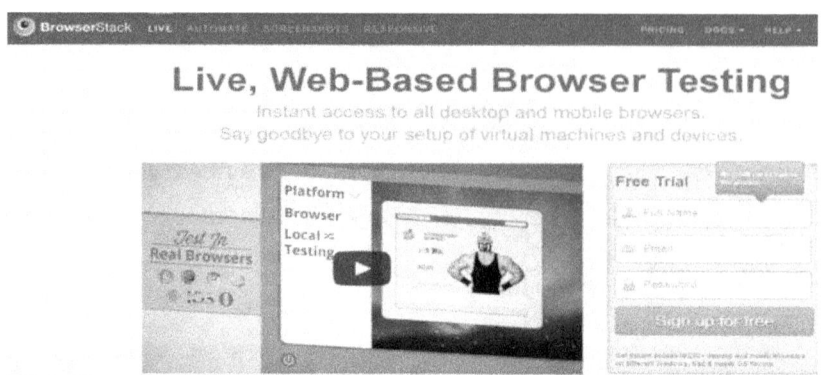

Visual Web Optimizer – Allows you to run A/B split testing on your website and track user analytics to learn from the results. When you are still beginning in your business, you don't really need this and it would be quite hard for you to understand its use. But as you grow and stay long enough, you will learn that optimizing the user experience is crucial for obtaining the best result and delivering the best product to your website for your visitors or viewers.

Support and User Feedback

While your business deals with interaction to customers, it is best to have some support management application available on your website. Even if you are building a web app, it is beneficial for you to have gather feedbacks from your audience as they know what's best for them. With enough testing and feedbacks, you can always improve any projects to be working as efficiently as possible.

Intercom – This app is an online service for handling user support problems. With a typical web-based helpdesk along with customer relationship management tools, Intercom is a perfect system for overseeing your project with clients or customers. Even a free social network can find Intercom useful for managing support questions. A free plan is also available and a great way to use with features and determine if it is indeed beneficial to your project.

UserVoice – can assist you in handling direct feedbacks. With a tiny widget set up on your site, visitors can directly send messages to your account as it works with a support system with organized backend tickets. If you are encountering problems that need support within a project, this tool can help you with it. Free plans are available indefinitely for one account.

TrackDuck – With the use of this powerful tool, you can set up a tiny box in one corner of your site where visitors may send feedback about the interface or bugs and any other issues they want to call your attention on.

Trackduck can easily integrate with other applications like Basecamp for tracking user feedback. A free edition of this app is available to provide all the basic services for one account. If you are just starting and want to test the waters, then this is a great tool for you.

CHAPTER 9: Tips to Improve Sales Performance

There's ample room for improvement on the internet and you will never know what works best until you test it. Meaning, the only way to discover what works well on your website is through constant testing and the best way to start increasing your sales. Here are some tests you can take and see what effects they can have on your business.

#1 - Offer Just one Product or Service on your Home Page

Are you selling multi-products on your websites? If you are and you're still not doing better, try selling just one product or service with more content describing the product and how it can be of use to the user. This way, you are educating the viewers. Giving more information about one product rather than providing them with more products and less information is not beneficial to them. That's why they don't stay much longer to click of the product you are offering on your website.

One way to see if this strategy works is to run the test for a week or two, then see if your sales increased.

#2 - Reposition you Opt-in Offers for List Building

Opt-in offers are usually used to build your list. Through your list, you will be able to connect with your subscribers regularly especially when you offer or launch a new product. Through your list, you are building a set of loyal customers. However, you need to know which part of your web page create the most impact on your customers and visitors.

If you don't have a rather lengthy sales letter, test by placing your opt-in offer on the top left of the page which the most prominent and mostly draws your viewer's eyes first. Or, you can also test placing your opt-in on the top fold of your home page. This is the area of the screen visible to a visitor before they scroll down the page.

If you are using a long letter for your opt-in offer, test by placing it on the second page or after you have grabbed your visitor's attention, establish your credibility by citing years of experience and encouraging testimonials from satisfied customers.

You can also test place your opt-in offer on every page of your site, so it's always in front of your visitors. The more sign–up opportunities you have, the more subscribers can get into your list.

#3 – Promote with Hover Ads

Are you familiar with hover ads? If you aren't, then maybe you are familiar with those small windows that suddenly pop-up once you visit a website. They contain special offers of information. Opt-ups have been useful to marketers before they were blocked by search engines. With this blocking software, visitors had missed a lot of information about some product which could have benefited them.

In lieu of pop-ups, hover ads replaced these pop-ups that behave like pop-ups but they are not real pop-ups so they were not blocked from the system. Test them on your website and you will see how. You can use these hover ads for special offers and see how much percentage of your sales had gone up.

#4 – Feature Product Benefits in your Headline

Headline usually creates an impact on your sales. It's because it's the first thing that visitors set their eyes into once they take a visit to your site. It catches a visitor's attention and compels him to read your sales letter.

#5 - Add Credibility to Enhance Visitor's Trust

Your sales copy must establish your credibility. One way to do this is to include customer testimonials. Make sure they come from genuine expressions of satisfied customers. It is more effective if the testimony elaborates on how the product or service had benefited the customer. This enhances your credibility more if it carries your experience and background. You must aim to convince the viewer or reader that you're the best person they can run to give the specific problems that need to be solved.

#6 – Focus on your Visitors

The most effective sales copy focuses on the viewer and not on you. Too often, the one writing the sales letter uses "I", "me" and "we" instead of "you" and "your."

CHAPTER 10: Elements of a Successful Business

There are 5 important key elements in online business that you need to focus on.

Choosing the Right Niche Market

Choosing the right niche is important in putting up your Internet Business. You can do some research on what most people want. You can also make a survey on your networks to determine their preferences. Study more about your competitors. Others even spied on their competitors' keywords just to be able to grab their page rank.

Currently, most people are interested in health, career, finance, success and business. By knowing what's trending in your network or knowing information related to your communities including their gender, age, locations, etc., you will be able to choose the best niche that will cater to their needs and wants.

Create a Professional Website

After determining your niche and identifying the types of people that are potential customers for your business, create a professional website by following instruction in Chapter 4. Remember how important it is to have a perfect workplace where you can connect with your market.

Offer Products or Services

After creating a great website or domain, make sure that you offer relevant products and service of high quality and value. Performance and quality count much in generating new visitors while retaining loyal customers. Enhancing your customer base depends on how you manage your online business.

Generate More Conversion

Visitors are important to your website but conversion is what makes your business successful. There are websites that generate a lot of traffic but fewer sales conversions. It is essential that you focus your marketing efforts on more targeted traffic that generate buyers and improve your sales. Improve your ads, keywords, offers, etc. Good sales copy to convert many of your visitors into paying customers.

Create System with Technology

If you lack the skill needs in doing some specific task while running your business like putting up your domain or writing relevant and exciting content, you can always outsource them. There are lots of freelancers out there who offer services like writing, designing or SEO services.

After establishing your business, you can improve your website by running it on automation or introduce affiliate marketing. If you don't have enough time to maintain your workplace, you can now have virtual assistant apps that will do administrative tasks for you.

One thing that you should not fail to have is an autoresponder that will send emails, answer queries and build your list automatically. Everything will just be connected to your email address. Auto responders like Aweber, Mailchimps, are just some that will benefit your business most.

Conclusion

Online business can be hard but not impossible. One can reach success through learning by personal observation, and from others who had been ahead in this journey. Like any other business, managing an online business is challenging and sometimes discouraging, but it will instill in you're a kind of character that only those who are diligent learners is worthy of.

Now that you have taken a little knowledge out of this eBook, we wish you would not fail to apply it in your own business until you attain real success. The more that you read, the more you will learn.

However, don't waste your time procrastinating, grabbing everything and losing your focus on what you have been trying to achieve…your GOAL!

Now that we have reached the end of this book, we leave everything you. It's time that you take a step forward regardless where you are at the moment – whether you're just starting or you had started!

Social Media Marketing 2017

Guide to Marketing Beyond the Search Engine

Table of Contents

Contents

INTRODUCTION 52

CHAPTER 1 – IMPORTANCE OF SOCIAL MEDIA MARKETING 53

CHAPTER 2 – REASONS FOR A FAILED SOCIAL MEDIA STRATEGY AND HOW TO FIX IT 56

CHAPTER 3 – SOCIAL MEDIA STRATEGIES FOR BOOSTING BRAND AWARENESS 59

CHAPTER 4 – KEY ELEMENTS FOR SOCIAL MEDIA MARKETING PLAN 70

CHAPTER 5 – OPTIMIZATION AND ONLINE BRAND DEVELOPMENT IN SOCIAL MEDIA MARKETING 72

CONCLUSION 74

Introduction

Social Media Marketing is one of the most talked about words for anyone who is looking to improve their online sales and presences, but is SMM (Social Media Marketing) all it's cracked up to be?

A lot of SMM companies are springing up these days all over the place and they're telling everyone that they will completely listen about how important the social medias such as YouTube, Twitter, Facebook, etc. are important to your business, but for the small and medium-sized businesses, does social media marketing necessary? Is spending additional expenses to hiring an SMM company truly worth it? Also, has anyone made their research on this matter before deciding to hire someone to develop their Facebook business page? Some of the SMM companies set up online things like the Facebook business pages for $500 to $1000, which is in fact can be accessed and made for free by anyone, as well as telling their clients that they won't be needing to have a website because Facebook is the largest social networking site around the globe and nearly everyone has their own Facebook account. While it's true that Facebook is the biggest social networking site in the world, and Facebook members are all potential customers, it doesn't guarantee that they're really buying. SMM companies are all happy in pointing out the positives and benefits of social media like how many people are using Facebook or the total number of tweets that was sent out in the previous year, and the number of people that watch videos in YouTube every day, but are you really getting the complete picture?

In this eBook, you will get a good consider Social Media Marketing in regards to selling and knowing if it works, who did it work for and if it did, why did Social Media Marketing work for them? And should business rely so heavily on social networks improved sales and online presence as a marketing strategy beyond search engine.

Chapter 1 – Importance of Social Media Marketing

In the world of technology, communication has now become much easier than ever. Our working has now shrunk from a wide populated land to networks of communicating individuals existing in a global village. People from around the world have come much closer together and the distances have greatly decreased to the extent that every individual is just a click away.

This is what social media as well as the developments in the online communication can do. An event in one place of the world can instantly reach other parts of the world in a matter of seconds. Just imagine if that event or news was about your business or organization. This significance of this innovation is the ease and comfort it provides. By using this technology at your advantage can greatly provide you a lot of benefits which include the following:

- **Brings you much closer to millions of people around the world without too much effort** – Practically, SMM is free. If you plan to reach out millions of people manually through physical means, you would need to make lots of investments. SMM is the best way available to efficiently reach out your potential prospects, not just in terms of finances but also of time as well.
- **There are possibilities for discovery of new prospects** – As you review your viewers' feedback, you might start seeing obvious patterns in your business response. People from certain regions, which you might never have thought of show much interest in your product, are your best customers. You will also be allowed by to see particular untapped markets that you may exploit. You can move swiftly and make use of the opportunity.
- **Promote your services or products as serious business** – SMM provides you the access virtually worldwide and all potential clients. People are there to share and read anything that you need to say. This will become your chance to build an image for your business that you are serious about the services or products that you provide.
- **Making you more accessible** – Social media websites make sure that you will gain exposure 24/7. In line with this, your clients will be able to drop off a message easily and you will be able to select a reply as soon as you wish. This will help in strengthening the body between you and your customer, and thus, inspiring a feeling of loyalty for your brand. But you will not find this consistent availability when you deal with a physical office because of the office closing and opening

times. This will be convenient for customers to reach out to you when they are in need and social media is the fastest way to reach out to one another.

- **Provides you feedback on type of viewers you have** – One of the most interesting things about SMM is the feedback level that you can get. As a matter of fact, through SMM you can get educated about the people who might be or are interested in your business services of products. This will provide you much better chances of changing your campaigns in order to gain much-improved results. You may also learn the number of people who are visiting your business page, or the ages of individuals who share or comment your posts, or event their localities, ethnicities, hobbies, religions, and preferences. You can get the world be aware of the existence of your product and services and at the same time educates you about the individuals who took great interest in it. You can get to know them much more through social media networks.

- **Your network is substantially growing** – The people who are added to your social network will become the cause for more people to join in. People that will keep adding the rate will grow with them. When the tree has branched out, your business will also grow.

- **More cost-effective and easier to manage** – Setting up a social media marketing campaign for brand awareness beyond the search engine will require you lesser effort as compared to when you plan to set out to traditional marketing campaign and execute your marketing campaign such as putting up advertisements, banners, and more, so as to get your message across. On the other hand, SMM is relatively easy to manage and frequently updated.

- **Your company will be seen as a person** – In general, most people do not prefer doing business with corporations or companies and they prefer working with individuals more. This is because a person is real, with a real presence in the world, someone whom you can relate to, and has thoughts, feelings, and emotions. Considering social media marketing for your brand will give it a human personification, and it will look more like an individual than a company, which is someone people can reach out to and can talk to, and thus, making a comfort zone between your company and the clients. It will then produce benefits for both of you.

- **Social media levels the playing field** – No matter if you are an individual startup or a multinational company, you will all be on the same level in the world of social media. Your resources and finances may not make any difference in terms of social media. But the different thing between one social media to another is the skill to attract and communication with people, as well as the quality of services or products that you are provided. On the other hand, startup companies face great financial difficulties to try promoting themselves, whereas the marketing of big corporations will continuously be dominating. Social media platforms will give you a fair playing field where you can show your skills and true spirit.

- **SMM brings worldwide popularity to your business name** – This will be your easy ticket to making an international level popularity. Your business or your name could become popular throughout the world with millions of fans and followers. Hundreds of millions of people can easily access social media sites where they come to express their views and communication online. Once you take advantage of the benefits of social media marketing, all of these individuals will instantly become your potential clients. Your business products or services will become a single search away.

Social media has been the new generation of information and communication transfer. Nearly all people keep visible of their online presence. You must not stay behind the competition and use this technology to your advantage.

Chapter 2 – Reasons for A Failed Social Media Strategy and How to Fix it

There has been an unbelievable reach of social media platforms and it has amazed entrepreneurs from all over the world. Both small and big businesses created accounts on social media sites and began to build a marketing strategy for various social media platforms. Nevertheless, while there are many partial methods to social media marketing, most businesses failed making a success to their marketing campaign. If you are among the business owners who failed connecting with the targeted audience and then engage them on social media platforms, introspection is the key. There are several reasons why your social media marketing (SMM) strategy failed and how you can fix it.

Failure to have understanding on customer behavior

Just as with any other marketing strategies, knowing your customers and how they behave is very important. A web designer or SEO will not be able to know the methods for building a marketing campaign on the social media by having an understanding about the customers' behavior. This why it is important to hire an SMM professional who can build a brand and making it famous among the targeted audiences.

Not having consistency

Even though you have a strong marketing plan with your first step being required to be a hit, if you do not have consistency with your social media marketing efforts, you will not have the capability to attain effective and long term results. It is among the greatest failures in SMM, and you can fix it by being committed to provide viral and engaging content across the year.

Putting the focus on your objectives and goals

Unlike the traditional methods of marketing, social media marketing is more about the wants of customers. Most social media marketers start their campaign by putting their focus on the business owner's goals. It would be a short-sighted approach to SMM because social media is not just about you. Thus, rather than focusing on you and your business goals, it is important to focus on the targeted market and their likes and dislikes.

Not working with the experts

SMM is not a joke or a job for children. Many companies assume that if they have accounts on Twitter, Facebook, and other social media platforms and as long as they put marketing messages and content on them, it would be more than enough to engage and connect with the audience. But it is far from the truth. There are lots of things that you should do to attain success on social media marketing. On the other hand, when you work with the experts, they will first do analysis on the market, conduct some research, and make proper strategies through assessment of the short term and long term implications.

Not listening or not considering the customer feedback and comments

It would be encouraging to see comments from the visitors on your posts. But if you cannot thank or follow up them for being interested in your brand, there will be a gap developed between you and your visitors. It is important to always make sure that there will be timely response provided to the feedback and comments of the visitors. 2-way communication is among the best advantages on social media sites and it must be used by marketers effectively.

Not spending enough money or time on social media marketing

Social media marketing is more affordable than the traditional marketing strategies, but it does not mean that there will be no investment to be done through money and time to attain the results you want. Rather than spending most of your marketing budget on traditional methods, it is great to consider putting in all your time and money on social media, because it is more effective, efficient, and more affordable. It is also reachable and will surely deliver visible results. To be able to get good returns on the time and money you invested, you should put in most of your marketing budget on SMM and get the performance monitored.

Relying on wrong performance metrics

It is another wrong approach is to measure the success of your SMM campaign on social media through the number of followers, likes, and fans. These are tricks that are only focused on increasing the numbers but it does not automatically get converted to customers. To be able to measure the success of the marketing campaign and your performance in a precise manner, you need to consider the elements that convert visitors like the number of retweets, shares, and more.

Not engaging users with your brand

Engaging with the users is essential in marketing. Engaging the customers with your brand is relatively easy, but there are still people who usually take it lightly and fail to engage the target audience with their brand. To be able to fix this up, the marketers must make sure that attractive, new, and engaging content will be posted on their social media profiles regularly. Making assessment on the marketing method of your competitors can also be helpful for you in coming up with effective methods to drive the traffic from your competitors to your own social media profiles.

So, next time you work on social media marketing strategies for your brand, it is important to be mindful of these mistakes to avoid them. There are several effective social media marketing strategies for boosting brand awareness through different social media platforms, including Twitter, Facebook, Instagram, and Snapchat. Read on to learn these strategies.

Chapter 3 – Social Media Strategies for Boosting Brand Awareness

Social media is an important that may exponentially increase your brand's visibility within an arena in which many people simply get lost in the crowd. It may be difficult to know where you should start when it comes to using social media platforms like Twitter, Facebook, Instagram, and Snapchat to increase brand awareness. Social media marketing help raise your profile, so it is a must for businesses to have a strong online presence. However, with most companies getting ahead of you with their knowledge with different platforms, these social media marketing strategies will help boost brand awareness for you through Facebook, Twitter, Instagram, and Snapchat. Learn how each of these platforms leverage your brand to getting to the peak and beyond the search engine.

a. **Facebook**

Facebook has still been the most valuable social media platform for online marketing. Because it has billions of active users, it is offering direct and unprecedented access to customers. Using this social media platform will require you to understand how Facebook works and how customers use this platform. As a major social media platform, you may face several challenges when trying to market your brand.

Building brand awareness from the scratch

All brands start out from scratch. It is essential to start building brand awareness by building a solid foundation. Put efforts to build a solid identity for your brand before moving into social media. As soon as you started using Facebook, you can now start reaching out to the community by targeting the demographics that have big possibility to use your products and/or services.

You may view people who follow your competitors, those who are quite interested in the same product or those who are in your geographic location. Your brand will certainly grow if you made a solid foundation and care for this foundation well. Building initial brand awareness on Facebook will take great amount of time, and necessitates momentum. If you stop building your brand, you may find yourself losing steam. Because of this, you must have a good idea about where you will go and how you will be able to get there from the scratch.

The use of incentives for increasing brand awareness

One way to increase brand awareness through Facebook is by using incentives. It can increase your presence in Facebook by 40%, because the nature of Facebook is for customers to share information. With attached incentives to your social media marketing campaign, you are leading the customers to feel like they are sharing something valuable. Incentives will depend on the involved company, such as free shipping, trials or samples, and discount coupons, among others, are all examples of valuable incentives that are most commonly shared.

To use incentives in a proper way, you will have to determine a low-cost offer to be provided to customers, which may be compelling to new customers. Nevertheless, you should also keep in mind that you should already have a strong brand identity when you offer incentives. You would also have to be ready for the incentives. You may experience a great traffic influx when the incentives really take off.

Running contests instead of straight promotions and marketing

Contests have its own way of driving people wild. As compared to incentives, which is quite costly, a contest often enables you to control the money to put out. When you create a contest like a simple free coffee for one year, you can gain a customer base. You only need to put in the initial work to get your contests out there, and the customers will instantly start to participate. You can even get more success in contests if you ask those who are signing up for the contest to refer friends to get more entries or as one of the requirement to join. This kind of promotion has high possibility of growing quickly, more particularly through a social media platform that is accessible and active like Facebook. Contests may not always lead to instant dollars, but it can improve your brand identity and increase brand exposure.

Keeping an eye on your statistics

It is essential to keep tabs of which social media marketing strategies through Facebook are doing well and which are not. You would want to put emphasis on the content to be shared. About 70% of customers trust a brand recommendation from friends, and there would only be 10% of prospects who would want to trust those that purely come from advertisements. Because of this, you need to focus on quality of the content you will share. But it is not always possible to know which content will become more famous.

The web may be a complicated place, so one of the best ways to determine the best campaigns is by keeping an eye on your statistics. In line with this, you can figure out which will work best for you and your brand. You may feel like you are trying lots of different things but you still do not get significant results in the beginning but you will see that you are developing a feel for the contents that will be famous.

Engaging with audience

Facebook really shines in the capability of engaging your audience regularly. With SMM through Facebook, you can speak to your prospects or current customers directly regarding the issues that matter to them. One important thing in general SMM, particularly in Facebook, is never neglecting this component. Most brands are receiving positive comments when they speak with their customers candidly and openly with regards to their products and services. There is nothing better than having positive comments and feedbacks for building a brand identity.

In addition, you may also consider studying your customers to see what they say about your brand on Facebook. This will offer unique capability for gathering information about what factors would add attraction to your brand and which of your Facebook SMM strategies work. It can even give you several insights to varying directions that you can take with your social media campaign.

While Facebook is the most popular social media platform these days, it is not the only important thing. A comprehensive brand awareness campaign will require different platforms working together to be able to make a targeted and cohesive strategy like Instagram.

b. **Instagram**

If you want to get your brand and products seen by more and more people, growing a strong following who relate to your brand is your magic spell. Instagram has now hundreds of millions of monthly users, which is more than Twitter, and so lots of brands find ways to interact with Instagram community and can earn invested customers to keep coming back for more in their offerings. However, it is not only the numbers that you must care about, but the people who are using this platform.

Instagram users are shoppers. About 70% of Instagram users have been reported to looking up a brand. If you post the right Instagram photos, customers will soak up your marketing message without any difficult sales pitches from you, and thereby, you can leverage from your magic spell to appeal to customers without a need to sell to them. If you are new to IG, no need to worry because all things you must know for marketing your brand is covered here. There are also more advanced tips for you.

Setting up your optimized business Instagram account

When making an account in Instagram, your business account needs to be separate from your personal account. Remember that social media marketing (SMM) is all about the audience and not about you, so keep all your snapshots and selfies from your travels with your loved one to remain personal. They do not have any relevance to your customers and it will not increase your sales.

As a matter of fact, your image should rarely appear in the IG page of your business, or not at all. The important things to include in your business account on IG are a link that will boost traffic to your website, interesting and informative Bio that will hook followers, and staying recognizable with a consistent photo and name. Hashtags and keywords will not really matter because they cannot be searched when they are on the bio. You will always be able to change your bio for the promotion of your latest sales, campaign, or launching, but do not ever forget a link.

Creating famous IG posts that other users would certain want to follow

A picture indeed is worth a thousand words, so leverage from the full power of hooking customers to your advantage through a photo. The increasing popularity of Instagram with its photo-centric platform gets 2x as many comments on posts that have image as compared to posts in other social media platforms that post just links or text.

One thing to keep in mind is avoiding hard selling to appeal to the social culture of IG. Photos enable viewers to make their own decisions without feeling pressure from the business, and remove the salesman aura from the scene. It is also advisable to promote your products and services with professional and creative photos. The power of product images was always important to shopping online, and the visual platform of IG is taking that power to the next level. IG is a social marketplace that can direct traffic into sales. It works by sharing photos that are unique, attention-grabbing, and full of personality.

Prioritizing professional quality

Do not post blurred or crop images because it can reduce your professionalism points. The format of Instagram makes your images automatically square. In line with this, consider the square shape when you select an image, or the entire appeal of the photo may be lost. Be sure your images will reflect professionalism, which requires you to post only high-quality images. A safe estimate to preserve the quality is by saving your photos at double resolution size.

Making unique lifestyle images that can capture your brand culture

Because your business Instagram account is not a direct sales market, you must put your focus on adding appeal and value to your news feed if you want to retain your followers and have more. The best party trick to inject your Instagram feed with appeal is through lifestyle images. You may use life-inspired scenes, backgrounds, and models to add a scene in your product. With this, users will most likely to image how great those products would look when they wear them out on a certain occasion.

In the marketing terms, do not present only the products and services that you offer, but also the lifestyle and culture that surround them to strengthen your brand equity. It would be the associated feelings with the brand. You may also post some suggestions on how to use or wear the products of your offering.

Offering exclusive announcements and promotions to followers

Just like Facebook, you should also pump your followers up with special offers, bonuses, and insider announcements on their feeds. Because more than 40% of IG users state that they follow or will be following a brand to take advantages of giveaways and benefits, it will give them that incentives. You can make use of text overlay so that you can include your promotion right on the image, and it has also been a visual and stylish way of announcing discounts and sales.

Reaching a wider IG following

Even if you have been posting amazing images, it is also important to have an Instagram social media marketing strategy to get people to start following you. You may include hashtags to increase your discoverability. You can also invite IG ambassadors to share your brand. Create a team of ambassadors who will spread the advantages of your brand to all their own followers. Encourage your followers to post reviews and photos to reach more users.

Another way to reach a wider Instagram following is by sharing the tagged photos on your own profile. It is a social media marketing bonus for you, which will save you lots of time because it basically hands over excellent images with just the tap of a screen.

Boosting customer engagement on Instagram

If an Instagram image has been shared and grew followers, but how will you be able to solidify that following into paying and loyal customers? It is through customer engagement. By closing the gap in communication between seller and buyer, IG is offering the chance to enhance your customer services, as well as receive any direct feedback from your customers, and even build relationships that may lead the visitors into loyal customers.

Keep in mind that the social nature of Instagram is to increase the more intangible aspects of social media marketing, such as brand equity, buyer loyalty, and lifetime user value. The associations and community of your brand are just as essential as your products and services, and IG is a platform that helps in promoting brand identity. Customers will soon come to you.

c. **Snapchat**

From 2015 to 2016, the monthly active users in Snapchat have doubled from a hundred million to 200 million of active users. It has shown essentially faster growth as compared to Twitter, Instagram, and Facebook. It has come a long way since its inception in year 2011 with its imaging sharing social media feature. Snapchat is among the best places for growing business. All you need is to know how to do it.

Everyday snaps to increase product and business knowledge

While it has a smaller impact on the bottom line of your business, it can do a great deal for you, more particularly if you are just getting started or if you have a unique product. Having daily snaps will help putting cement on your business within the top-of-mind awareness of your followers. They can also increase your Snapchat's value because followers want to see more than just a collection of carefully taken discount codes and product shots.

Several ideas for the daily content on Snapchat are videos highlighting the culture of your business, behind-the-scenes images, or Snaps that show different ways to use your products or several features. Take advantage of the drawing tools and filters for crafting engaging and creative snaps. Consistently posting will help you inform your followers of various products, providing more familiarity with your business. This can increase the possibility of turning them into sales and loyal customers in the future.

Snapchat-exclusive promotions for increasing e-commerce sales

Promotions on snapchat rely on your business that has already growing Snapchat following. The more followers you have, the more possible customers you can reach. Aside from your everyday snaps, you may include occasional codes and discounts. The main purpose of this strategy is by converting your followers into sales. But it also serves a long-term and secondary purpose. You will be able to advertise Snapchat discounts on your other social media accounts to be able to grow your list of followers on Snapchat.

Q & A on Snapchat to create meaningful relationships with followers

Even though it may seem hard, hosting a Q & A on Snapchat is one great way of taking an established Snapchat following and be converted into sales. You can set a time and date to host your Q & A and then encourage your followers to send in questions and on your other social media platforms. Snapchat videos are good for this. Allowing advanced question submission will ensure that you would not have a shortage of questions when you finally air your Q & A.

If you got too many questions, just choose the best or the most appropriate among all the questions, but keep in mind that not all questions should be related to your product or business. Keep some less serious questions as a chance to show off your personality. Read out the question and shout out the author when you answer. This will make them feel recognized and thus, creating a personal connection to your brand.

These are just few but very effective tips to grow your business in social media marketing through Snapchat. Learn more tips on Twitter SMM.

d. **Twitter**

Twitter is another very effective tool to increase brand awareness. It helped lots of people in growing their business. With more than a hundred million people on the social network each day, it has been among the major social media marketing platform for business success. There are several things that you need to keep in mind to become successful in social media marketing through Twitter.

Picking the right times

Your customers have a time when using Twitter. Test out various times to figure out when they use Twitter. One good sign that your audience is most available is when your posts gets comments, likes, and retweets. You may also check your competitors and see when they usually post and how much engagement they are receiving on various kinds of posts during different times of the day.

Finding your keywords

To leverage from social media marketing through Twitter and promote your brand successfully, you should master the art of using and finding the right keywords. Keywords are ultimately important to SMM, because they can help increase your tweets' popularity by making your posts easier to categorize and find.

All the better news is that you will be able to conduct the right keywords and key phrases through simple search from your Twitter account. For instance, when you search for writing job, you may also find other keywords like freelance writing, writer, freelance jobs, content writing, content writer, blogger, and more. Be sure to keep a list of the best keywords for your business and you should use them for creating buzz around your brand.

Being consistent

No matter if you have great content to share with your followers, have a professional Twitter account, and/or a quality product that you can pitch, you will not succeed in your social media marketing campaign if you are not consistent. Do not tweet every 2 days or once a week. You should tweet each day. The goal of using Twitter is by engaging quality content with your audience, which has relevance to your brand and which adds value to the lives of your followers, helping your audience like, know, and trust you. You will only be able to do this when you are present in their online lives.

Harnessing hashtags

Hashtags are used for marketing topics or keywords in a tweet. With a hashtag, you are categorizing your tweet so that people can easily found it, and this does not only make it simpler for people to find your tweets, but you will also be able to improve follower engagement. You can use popular and current hashtags. You can also create your own or jump on other Twitter users' bandwagon and use a trending tag to attract people to your posts.

Selecting a catchy name

Choose a professional name that your followers and prospects can remember and relate to. It should be a name that is irresistible that Twitter people cannot help but follow. You should keep it relevant and it is important to include at least some parts of your business name. It can be the abbreviated version or other things that come to your mind. But keep it short.

Chapter 4 – Key Elements for Social Media Marketing Plan

As with any business marketing strategies, you need to have a plan for success and utilizing social media is no different. For you to effectively use social media as one viable business marketing strategy, you need to have a secured plan in place. Just as having a business marketing plan, you need to have a marketing plan for utilizing social media. Therefore, when you're writing a plan to get social, you must consider the most important element to ensure your business success. After all, there is nothing worse than wasting both your time and efforts on something that is simply not useful or beneficial for your business. Social media is now considered as one of the most effective tool for businesses when used in the right way.

Here are the top 5 most important elements you need to consider in your social media business marketing plan:

1. **Business Objective** – First and foremost, you need to figure out what's your overall goal to using many different communication channels online. You can use the social media platforms to build your brand online, sell a service or a product, or get to interact without the customer base. No matter what you goal is, your content should be aligned with your objectives. Your main reason for being in the business is to effectively address a problem or solve it held by a specific number or group of people, for example, you target audience. Therefore, your online strategy should also tackle the needs and wants of your target audience.

2. **Media Outlets to Utilize** – There are a lot of online platforms to choose from. However, it's very important to know which of the social media platforms are best for your business as well as for your target demographic. Identifying which platform to use is a primary source of the contemplation for a lot of small business owners. One of the best ways to get a clear understanding of what social media platform to use for your business, you need to figure out where your potential clients and prospects hang out. The easiest way to achieve this is by having a survey that simply asks your followers about the top 3 social media websites that they use. It's much easier to have this kind of information upfront than spending your time in using the social media platform where you will get just a few following or engagement.

3. **Engaging Content** – Have you ever heard of the saying that "content is king"? This also applies to using social media sites as well. Your content needs to be

educated and can inspire a response and a reaction. It's crucial to provide the necessary information to your audiences in a compelling and unique way. Of course, regardless of what industry you are in, there are hundreds and thousands of people sharing the same information on similar subject, that's why you need to identify a way to stand out as well as make your content unique and unforgettable.

4. **Customer Policy** – Customer service can make or break the reputation of your company. Your customers should get a feeling that they are valuable to your business for them to continue buying your services or products. It's also the same with using social media; your followers should get the feeling that you are completely willing to provide help and assistance about their needs. Using social media sites for marketing should include a plan on how you will handle your customer complaints and concerns online. In addition to that, you need to assign someone who will be responsible for the entire online communications of your business and have the know-how about getting engaged with current customers as well as with potential customers.

5. **A System for Measuring Outcomes** – When it gets right to it, success should be measured for your business to grow. Your social media plan needs to include certain types of metric to gauge the effectiveness as it relates to your entire online objective and goals. You need to identify how well you've achieved the first things you set to do. Were your goals to achieve a certain amount of sets every quarter or each month met? Did you utilize new sales tactic or promotion? How well did they work? Were your goals to achieve a certain number of fans or followers met? Did you meet your goals or fall short? Based on how well you meet your goals, you need to provide you company a grading in order determine the room for improvement. Having the measuring system for outcomes will help you in determining how well or effective your plans are.

Social media is without a doubt a viable tool for marketing but needs not to be the only marketing strategy you will use if you desire having a sustainable business growth. To make your business achieve success, you need to plan your social media business marketing just as your do with anything else.

If you don't have a plan about how to use online networks, you should make one based on the business objectives you desire you company to achieve online. If you have a marketing plan, just review it carefully for effectiveness.

Chapter 5 – Optimization and Online Brand Development in Social Media Marketing

Online marketing has never been as easy as we expect it to be, more particularly in terms of branding and working within a budget. In this case, you must pay attention to all details and resources about how you would market your online business. The wrong processes will lead to wasting money and time, and outstanding online marketing strategies will provide increase conversions and online exposure. Social media marketing became a famous alternative for online business branding. Companies are not thinking of social media sites as websites for children. They are now valuable networking and online marketing resources for business.

Getting started

Before you get started in SMM, you must nip the urge of joining each social media platform. It is not hurtful to have online presence everywhere, but there is not advantage in wasting time when you set up a social media account that is not active. The website owner may delete it or it may have been outdated and looked unprofessional. Also, there is no way to work them unless you have some help. You should also have a plan of action to be able to position your company correctly from the start.

Proper setup

It is important to learn how to setup and position your company with the best social media marketing platforms like Facebook, Twitter, Instagram, and Snapchat. Among the significant initial positioning details that you consider, including selecting the right username for your profile links, identifying which are the best social media marketing platforms for your interests and niche, selecting the most attractive media and profile information to share, establishing a time schedule that permits working as many networks as possible, developing a skill for some filtering activity in accordance to the appropriate social media site, and more.

Implementing

A predefined SMO strategy should be include, expediting the professional results that you need for your business. It is easy to assume that social media marketing is just setting up social media networks and marketing, but while it is a part of the process, social networking is not involved in SMM. The key to this offsite marketing process is content, like articles, discussions, videos, blogs, images, link, and other things that social media marketing needs to correspond with the SEO.

Social networking and online brand development may seem easy but it is not a simple process. There are defined strategies that must include both social media marketing and search engine optimization to be able to build a process called social media optimization. Generating social media marketing will help you learn how to brand your business online properly and lead your business to sure success in the social media.

Conclusion

Are you tired of spending many hours on social media and do not know if it is working? This guide helps online marketers to learn more about leveraging the power of social media marketing. A business will almost not be able to survive in the world without online marketing. The best thing about it is that social media marketing is effective, cost-effective, and can work for anyone.

Any businesses, not matter how small or big, will be able to market its brand online through social media marketing. Make sure to have a comprehensive social media marketing plan before starting to consider how every social media platform among Facebook, Twitter, Snapchat, and Instagram, can enhance your business, and you would not go far wrong.

The End

www.ingramcontent.com/pod-product-compliance
Lightning Source LLC
Chambersburg PA
CBHW081213180526
45170CB00006B/2325